Healing

is coming!

Healing

is coming!

Don Egan

RSVP Trust

P O Box 55, Stowmarket, Suffolk, IP14 1UG, England

ISBN-13 978-0-9554390-2-5
ISBN-10 0-9554390-2-7

Published by
The RSVP Trust
P O Box 55, Stowmarket, Suffolk, IP14 1UG, England

What others are saying...

"Don Egan is one of Britain's best kept secrets. He's the kind of guy who just gets on with it - without any hype or fuss. But the results of his ministry have been absolutely remarkable. Truth is, God has used Don to see some of the most incredible miracles I have personally ever heard about. A man of profound integrity with a deep love for Christ and an unwavering compassion for people - this book isn't written by a theorist but a practitioner. As you read it, it will undoubtedly stir greater faith and inspire you to experience God's healing and wholeness in your own life as well as in the lives of others."

Rev Roy Todd
International healing evangelist

"My friend Don Egan teaches Biblical principles clearly and simply for healing, health and well-being and don't we need it?"

Canon J.John
Philo Trust

"I'm at a loss. Whenever I speak with people who are sick and need encouragement, a faith injection or a miracle – I give them Don Egan's *A Word About Your Healing*. Don has an incredible, accredited healing ministry. Now that he has put so much of what he knows and practices into this fabulous book, we are all out of excuses for not just passing on books but actually practicing what Jesus preached and seeing what he saw – healing is coming!"

Anthony Delaney
Writer, Broadcaster, Leader of Ivy Manchester

Don Egan's latest book *Healing is Coming* is challenging, controversial and provocative and needless to say not everyone will agree with everything in it. It is however supremely pastoral - written by a gentle man with a big heart to see God's children walk in the fullness of their inheritance. I gladly commend it."

Greg Downes
Director, Centre for Missional Leadership
London School of Theology

contents

"The tongue that brings healing is a tree of life,
but a deceitful tongue crushes the spirit."

Proverbs 15:4

Chapter 1

Healing is coming!

I believe three things are going to happen as you read this book. I call them the 3 'R's:

1. Reinforce - you will read about something you already know and are already doing. That's no bad thing. Do golfing world champions still practise their golf? Of course they do!

2. Remind - you will be reminded of something. Something you know but are not doing.

> "So I will always remind you of these things, even though you know them and are firmly established in the truth you now have."
>
> 2 Peter 1:12 (NIV)

3. Reveal - hopefully you will experience a revelation. Something you don't know and are not doing.

It is no accident that you are reading this book. I believe God has put this book into your hands for a purpose. This is a divine appointment. So many lie sick instead of fulfilling their God-ordained potential. Many, if not most, churches avoid the healing issue through fear. Perhaps you will read something in these pages that will make a difference to you and to others.

Several years ago, I was speaking at some open-air meetings in Rwanda. Every night we prayed for the sick. One night, as I was speaking out words of faith over the crowd, I said these words, 'Sickness is going! Healing is coming! Now!'

I don't know why I said it, other than that faith was rising up in my heart. Although they are just words, I felt in my spirit that this was a direct challenge to sickness and something was happening in the spiritual realm which, in turn, caused physical healing to occur in people's bodies. We had many testimonies of healing during those meetings.

In this book, I want to share why, right now, I believe that sickness is going and healing is coming. As you read this book, don't be surprised if sickness starts to go and healing starts to come. It often just takes a word to cause a miracle to happen.

> "When evening had come, they brought to him many who were demon-possessed and he cast out the spirits *with a word*, and *healed all* who were sick."
>
> Matthew 8:16

I am aware that there is a lot of rubbish talked

about the healing ministry, which has no basis in scripture. Little bits of folklore have built up around the healing ministry, which, in reality, just get in the way. As we go through this book I want to clear away some of that rubbish so we can see clearly God's view on healing.

> "Then Judah said, 'The strength of the labourers is failing, and there is so much rubbish that we are not able to build the wall.'"
> Nehemiah 4:10

In this book I want to lay a clear biblical foundation so you can build your faith and get a healing breakthrough in your life and the lives of those around you.

Sometime ago my friend Jane asked me to pray with her Dad, Brian, who had prostate cancer. Brian had taken part in a PSA test (Prostate Specific Antigen count), which tests for the presence of cancer in the prostate. If the test is below 5, no action is required. However, Brian's result was 8.7. He went on to have a biopsy and out of 10 sites, 2 were positive for cancer. The doctors felt they couldn't operate because surgery would cause too much damage. A further PSA test showed things were getting worse, as the result was now 18.5. This was very serious. At this point, Brian read a few books on Christian healing, including my book, *A Word about your Healing*.

I went to Jane's house to pray with her Dad, along with Jane and her sister Lindsey. We shared communion and prayed for Brian. As we laid hands on Brian, I cursed the cancer and we asked, as Brian requested, that the doctors would carry out a further PSA test.

Brian felt invigorated by the time of prayer but wanted to know what the results of a further test would be. Several weeks later, a further PSA test was carried out and the result was 0.1 - as low a reading as is possible! There was no sign of cancer in Brian's body. We give God thanks and to him be all the glory!

A couple of years ago, I was speaking one weekend at a church near Blackpool. On Sunday night I ministered to those who came forward for healing. Several people said they had been touched by God at the time, and a lady with severe back pain told me the pain seemed to have gone.

After I got back home, the vicar sent me an email a few days later, to tell me that a lady called Irene, who had been blind, had suddenly recovered her sight as she left the church that night. She had not seen her daughter's face for many years and had never seen her granddaughter's face but now she could see them clearly.

The following year I spoke at a Christmas Carol Service on the seafront at the Marine Hall near Blackpool. After the service, I met Irene and she told me the whole story, which was even more surprising!

She had been registered blind for 25 years. During that time, when she closed her eyes she saw a white light. But six months before the healing service, she closed her eyes one night and she saw a man's face. She didn't know what to make of this but from that day she saw the same face whenever she closed her eyes.

On the night of the healing service I spoke at, she came forward for prayer. Nothing happened, so she went back to her seat. At the end of the service she was in the foyer and a friend led her over to where I was standing to say goodbye. As I shook her hand, her eyes were opened and she saw my face. It was the face she had seen every day for six months previously when she'd closed her eyes. She was speechless and couldn't tell anyone but went home, knelt down, and thanked Jesus for healing her.

As she told me the story I was astonished. We tend to think healing from God will be all neat and make sense - come for prayer, we pray, healing comes. But it rarely happens how or when we think it will. God does things differently but his word is powerful to work his works.

> "'For my thoughts are not your thoughts,
> nor are your ways my ways,' says the LORD.
> 'For as the heavens are higher than the earth,
> so are my ways higher than your ways,
> and my thoughts than your thoughts.
> So shall my word be that goes forth from my mouth;
> it shall not return to me void,
> but it shall accomplish what I please,
> and it shall prosper in the thing for which I sent it.'"
> Isaiah 55:8, 9, 11

Recently, I was speaking at another weekend healing mission in Blackpool. On the first night I noticed an elderly lady in the prayer line. As I approached her a member of the church was already praying with her. 'It's her spine,' he said. We laid hands on her back and commanded every disc to be restored and properly aligned. She left the meeting without comment. She came back the next night and told me, 'The doctors told me my spine is disintegrating. Every night, for the last four years, I have had to get up every hour through the night to take a hot shower to ease the pain. But last night, after you prayed, I slept through the night for the first time in four years!'

In the same meeting, another lady reported that she had bashed her knee very badly weeks before and had been limping ever since. The pain was so bad. But, as we prayed on the first night, her knee was instantly healed.

Another lady said that her hearing had been impaired in one ear. As we prayed, her ear 'popped' and she could hear. She didn't want me to share this until she confirmed it was permanent. She wrote to me a week later to confirm her hearing was still clear.

In Manchester a lady came forward on crutches with terrible pain in her ankles. As I prayed for her, she fell to the floor under the power of God. She later wrote to me to tell me that as I prayed, she felt something like 'shackles' on her ankles shattering. The pain has gone and she doesn't need the crutches any more.

Another lady at the same meeting had excruciating pain in her hips, so that even dressing was extremely painful. After we prayed, the pain subsided and she can now get dressed without any pain. To God be all the glory!

I share these stories of healing so that you

may be encouraged and know that sickness is going and healing is coming.

If you read the life of Jesus in the four gospels, you won't find him teaching much about healing. He teaches people about the kingdom of God, of which healing is a part. But there is such an ignorance of faith and healing in our day that there is an urgent need for teaching on this subject. It is a matter of life and death.

> "My people are destroyed for lack of knowledge."
>
> Hosea 4:6

Indeed, there is also today, the preaching of a watered-down gospel that restricts the work of Jesus to the forgiveness of sin only. In some places it doesn't even include that.

Amazing though the central work of Christ on the cross is, the gospel of Jesus includes far more than dealing with our sinful past. He came to give us a better future and life in abundance!

Soren Kierkegaard said, 'The Church has performed a greater miracle than Jesus: Jesus turned water into wine. The Church has taken the wine of the gospel and turned it into the water of human religion.' I want to look afresh at a part of the gospel and the kingdom that is often ignored or overlooked. Yet this aspect of the kingdom of

God was an integral part of the ministry of Jesus and the early disciples.

I pray that God will speak to you through this book and that sickness will go and healing will come as you read it.

Chapter 2

God wants you well!

People are often confused about suffering and sickness: 'Doesn't God allow suffering to build up our faith?' It's important to understand the difference between suffering and sickness. I may suffer difficulties in my relationships, my finances, my job or may even suffer persecution. In the long-term these things can build character.

> "Not only so, but we also rejoice in our sufferings, because we know that suffering produces perseverance; perseverance, character; and character, hope."
>
> Romans 5:3, 4 (NIV)

The word 'sufferings' is translated from the Greek *'thlipsis'* which has the meaning: tribulation, trouble, anguish, persecution, burdened, pressure, and distress. These words refer to life's difficulties and not to sickness. For sure, trouble and suffering has often resulted in enriching life on earth.

Billy Graham wrote, 'Comfort and prosperity have never enriched the world as adversity has done. Out of pain and problems have come the sweetest songs, the most poignant poems, the most gripping stories. Out of suffering and tears have come the greatest spirits and the most blessed lives.'

Notice he does not use the word 'sickness' here.

Suffering is not the same as sickness. Sickness is a curse and oppression from the devil. When God was telling his people how to walk in blessing and avoid being under a curse, he said:

> "However, if you do not obey the LORD your God and do not carefully follow all his commands and decrees I am giving you today, all these curses will come upon you and overtake you."
>
> Deuteronomy 28:15

Then God listed the curses, which included sickness. Sickness came into the world when men and women rejected God and stepped out of the protection of his blessing.

Sickness is also oppression from the devil. It is not a 'tool' that God uses to grow our character.

> "...how God anointed Jesus of Nazareth with the Holy Spirit and with power, who went about doing good and healing all who were oppressed by the devil, for God was with

him."

Acts 10:38

God does not send curses or sickness, or oppress his people in order to make them grow. But he may allow life's difficulties to tarry for a while for the growth of our character.

Sometimes I cringe when I hear people say, 'Well, if God chooses to heal me, great. If not, I'll just have to pray for patience.'

I've got some good news for you – God has chosen to heal you. As far back as the second book of the Bible, God revealed that he wants you to be well.

"... I am the LORD, who heals you."

Exodus 15:26

'Well, if that's true, why am I still sick?' We need to understand why we can be healed. You know, God is not some sort of religious magician who floats around spreading a few bits of magic here and there. Some people talk as though God was like a magician with a little magic wand.

No, God exchanged a contract to set you free. It was a contract signed with the blood of his Son on a Roman cross of execution. On that cross, where the blood of God and the blood of man mingled down the body of Jesus, a divine exchange took place. Jesus took our sin and gave us forgiveness. He took our poverty and gave us his riches. He took our punishment and gave us freedom. And he took our sickness and gave us healing.

> "He took up our infirmities and carried our diseases."
>
> Matthew 8:17

As someone who has watched his own son die, I can tell you God did not do that lightly. Even though he must have known that Jesus would later rise from the dead, I am absolutely sure that God's pain and grief was deeper than mine, when I wept over my son's dead body. God hates sickness and death. He loathes them both.

So now we need to receive the work of the cross. We need to receive Jesus personally into our lives. We need to say sorry for the past and receive what he did on the cross. His healing is our inheritance. In order to receive our inheritance someone has to die. So some people think they can't be healed till they go to heaven. No, it's not we who have to die. Jesus has already died to complete the terms of the inheritance.

Yes, we have an Enemy who doesn't want us to benefit from our inheritance in Christ. But, as with an earthly inheritance, once we are sure what we have inherited, we begin to enforce the contract, so we receive what was given to us legally. So we must enforce the work of the cross. Christ paid for my healing. He gave it to me. Therefore I must declare that I receive it, expect it and will enforce it. We enforce it by faith, by reciting the words of the contract.

"...by his wounds we are healed."

Isaiah 53:5

We have to say what we want. We have to speak the solution not the problem. Sounds stupid? Well, the Bible tells us to say what we want, not what we have.

"Let the weak say, 'I am strong.'"

Joel 3:10

Some people have accused me of condemning those who don't have enough faith. But this is not my intention. This verse from Joel makes it clear that, as far as faith is concerned, it is in our hands.

The Bible tells us that each of us has a measure of faith:

"...God has dealt to each one a measure of faith."

Romans 12:3

Jesus told us that even with very small

amounts of faith we can move mountains (Matthew 17:20). The Bible teaches that we can increase our faith by hearing the word of Jesus (Romans 10:17).

So as far as faith is concerned, it is up to us to keep it topped up. I am no different to you or anyone else. I have to keep my faith topped up. I do have periods where faith runs low but I put myself in a place where I can hear God's word and faith increases.

God wants you well. But you need to engage with the contract on his terms to see a breakthrough. Your healing was purchased with the blood of Jesus. We need to meditate on the blood and all Jesus purchased for us. We need to humble ourselves under the mighty hand of God and he will lift us up in due season. Sickness is going! Healing is coming! Now!

Chapter 3

The roots of sickness

Why is there sickness in the world? If God is a loving God and he created the world, why is there sickness? This is the great question that mankind has tried to answer down the ages. Some suggest God is not loving but angry. Others suggest God is loving but not powerful enough. The truth is a little different.

God created the world, and you and me, out of his goodness and greatness. Like all living things, there are conditions that cause us to thrive and conditions that cause us to suffer. So God set out the parameters of how we could live well and happily. The key condition was to live in a close relationship with God.

In Genesis chapter 3 we read that our ancestors chose to step outside of this blessing and thus separated themselves from God's blessing and protection.

One of the words for sickness is 'disease'. This word gives us a clue to the roots of sickness. In the Garden of Eden there was an ease to life. Everything was provided and everything was beautiful. No sickness, death or pain.

However, once our ancestors separated themselves from their relationship with God, they lost that ease. Their peace evaporated and they had 'dis-ease'.

I believe the foundational root of all sickness is that, deep down in our spirit, we are not at ease with our Creator.

I do not mean that if you are sick you are especially sinful. Not at all. What I mean is that the human race was corrupted in the act of rebellion in the Garden of Eden. It sowed a seed in every soul descended from that moment.

So we live in a fallen world. What we have is not the world God planned for us but a world 'ill at ease' with itself - a dis-eased world. And I use those words intentionally.

Also, I am not saying that God only heals those who repent and turn to him. He clearly heals some who go on to reject him even after they are healed.

But if you want to be restored and made completely whole, you need to understand the condition of human life on earth.

As my good friend J John often says, 'The heart of the human problem is the problem of the human heart.' I like that.

If you think of all the suffering and pain in the world, you have to realise that the vast majority of it is caused by man's inhumanity to man. It is rooted in the problem of sin in the human heart.

The evangelist Billy Sunday once wrote to the mayor of an American town requesting a list of people who needed help and prayer. The mayor sent him the city directory with everybody's names in it!

Our separation from God is the root of all the trouble in the world. Paul, writing to the Roman believers, painted a picture of the whole of creation 'groaning' for the full work of God to be completed.

> "For we know that the whole creation groans and labours with birth pangs together until now."
>
> Romans 8:22

In the following verses he also says that believers groan for that day and even the Holy Spirit groans for that day.

So even those of us who repent of our past and turn to Christ and are born again, still have the potential to do great evil, if we neglect our relationship with God. The human heart, if neglected, will run to sin as surely as an untended garden runs to weeds.

Billy Graham once famously declared, 'I know my own heart and its deceitful power. I know that outside of the restraining grace of God, there is no evil act I could not commit within 30 minutes of leaving the platform.'

The human spirit is the battleground of the forces of good and evil. The long shadow cast by sin across the human race is the source of our dis-ease. Even if we understood all the medical evidence of any physical disease or infirmity, I believe the true root of all sickness is the separation of our spirit from our Creator. But let me repeat, my dear friend, it is not our 'sins' – plural – that create dis-ease but 'the sin' of the world - singular.

> "The next day John saw Jesus coming toward him, and said, 'Behold! The Lamb of God who takes away the sin of the world!'"
> John 1:29

'The sin' is our rejection of God and his Son. It is this sin that leads to all other sins.

In addition to our own proclivity to rebel against God, we have to understand that we have a ferocious Enemy who wants to wipe out God's creation and us along with it. We would do well to understand his role in sickness and disease as well.

Chapter 4
The Enemy who kills

> "The thief comes only to steal and kill and destroy; I have come that they may have life, and have it to the full."
> John 10:10 (NIV)

If you do an internet search for the word 'healing' you will get thousands of results and many that have no link to Christ or the Bible. There are all sorts of weird and wonderful claims to healing from spiritualists, mediums, hypnotists and those who claim they have 'the gift'.

For every blessing of God and every miracle he does, we need to be aware of the counterfeit sent by Satan. Some Christians are surprised that I include hypnotism in such a list. There isn't room in these pages to fully explain why I believe Christians should avoid hypnotism, but I have written a detailed explanation in my book *Spiritual Detox.*

Whilst you may get a 'cure' through some of these things, you may well get some unexpected 'side-effects'.

We expect to find Satan involved in the occult and witchcraft and he knows that. Sometimes he comes to us in disguise to trap us by making us think something is good and helpful, when actually it will trap us, destroy us or lead us away from Jesus.

> "Satan himself masquerades as an angel of light."
>
> 2 Corinthians 11:14 (NIV)

It is important therefore to ask questions about those offering any sort of healing ministry.

1. Is it biblical?
2. Is it centred on Jesus?
3. Is it rooted in the Christian Church?
4. What is the fruit of it? (Matthew 7:20)

Some of the 'healing' on offer is described by some as 'New Age'. This title is misleading as it tends to be old paganism repackaged. It was ever so. Centuries ago the apostle John warned believers of such things.

> "Dear friends, do not believe every spirit, but test the spirits to see whether they are from God, because many false prophets have gone out into the world. This is how you can recognise the Spirit of God: Every spirit that acknowledges that Jesus Christ has come in the flesh is from God, but every spirit that

does not acknowledge Jesus is not from God. This is the spirit of the antichrist, which you have heard is coming and even now is already in the world."

1 John 4:1-3 (NIV)

Unbelief in the Church

Even when we come to the Christian Church we can see the effect of Satan's deception. So many churches have nothing to do with healing, despite it being an integral part of the gospel of Jesus Christ. One lady wrote to me after listening to me talk about healing on my podcast. 'I've been a Christian for 20 years and never heard any teaching on healing,' she wrote.

Whenever I speak about the subject of healing in churches, there are always people who need healing. They don't all come for prayer but even those who don't, often confide in me afterwards that they wanted to.

We pray so often, 'Your kingdom come, your will be done on earth as it is in heaven.' There is no sickness in heaven and therefore Jesus taught us to pray that the same would be true on earth. And yet so many in the Church are sick. Why?

Paul touched on one reason when writing to the believers at Corinth.

> "For this reason many are weak and sick among you, and many sleep."
> 1 Corinthians 11:30

So the same was true in Paul's day – there were many who were sick among the believers. Paul says there was a reason for this.

> "But let a man examine himself, and so let him eat of the bread and drink of the cup. For he who eats and drinks in an unworthy manner eats and drinks judgement to himself, not discerning the Lord's body."
> 1 Corinthians 11:28, 29

Paul tells them that the reason there are sick people in Church is because they are 'not discerning the Lord's body.'

Today, pretty much all who call themselves Christian believe that Jesus' sacrifice – his body and blood – paid for their forgiveness. Yet, so many of the same people say that God doesn't heal today or they are not sure if it's God's will to heal everyone.

To me that's like saying, 'It's not God's will to forgive everyone.' But the Bible says that God "desires all men to be saved and to come to the knowledge of the truth" (1 Timothy 2:4).

Scripture is shot through with statements that the new covenant in Jesus' blood not only paid for our forgiveness but also abundant life, which includes peace, protection, provision and healing.

Isaiah tells us, "...by his stripes we are healed."

Isaiah 53:5

That is, by his wounds.

Matthew tells us, "He himself took our infirmities and bore our sicknesses" Matthew 8:17.

Yet today, so many believe Jesus came like a bus conductor giving out tickets for heaven, which he paid for. What he did on the cross was so much more than purchase a place in heaven for you. His body and blood purchased a place in the New Covenant, where all God has he shares with you.

> "Christ has redeemed us from the curse of the law, ...that the blessing of Abraham might come upon the Gentiles in Christ Jesus..."
>
> Galatians 3:13,14

The blessing of Abraham is the covenant that God made with Abraham to release the blessing of heaven. The Enemy is powerless against this covenant unless he can deceive and confuse you. If he can minimise the covenant or convince you it's only applicable in the hereafter, he will rob you of your healing and your blessing.

It is a testament to the effectiveness of Satan's deception that so many in the Church don't believe we can get healed today.

Be careful today that you are rightly "discerning the Lord's body" – that you understand the breadth and depth of his love towards you. That you understand that his will for you is to be healed and set free from every curse Satan throws at you.

> "It is for freedom that Christ has set us free. Stand firm, then, and do not let yourselves be burdened again by a yoke of slavery."
>
> Galatians 5:1

'There's a war on!' My Dad used to say that when we ran short of anything when I was growing up. At the time I didn't find it funny. But as I grow older I realise that, when he was a teenager during World War 2, he must have heard that many times during the government rationing. The threat was that England should become Germany's slave. But, by the victory of our forces, we were set free from slavery. So too, Jesus has set us free from Satan's slavery.

> "For this purpose the Son of God was manifested, that he might destroy the works of the devil."
>
> 1 John 3:8

I'm telling you that the devil wants you

dead. If he can't kill you he wants you seriously incapacitated, addicted or, at the very least, distracted.

Obviously, injury or sickness may happen through natural causes, like an accident or our environment, but when it does you can be sure Satan and his minions will be there to make matters worse.

The spirit of infirmity

> "And behold, there was a woman who had a spirit of infirmity eighteen years, and was bent over and could in no way raise herself up."
>
> Luke 13:11

I am learning that there are two levels of sickness at work in people's bodies. There is the physical problem in a person's body – whatever the sickness or disease is – but there is also a spiritual level. The Bible calls it the 'spirit of infirmity'.

The spirit of infirmity is a demonic spirit that oppresses people in their body. Now let me say, first of all, not all our sickness begins with a demonic attack. If you've eaten too many hamburgers all your life, and you end up with a weak heart, that's not the devil, that's too many hamburgers.

If you trip and twist your ankle – that's not the devil, you just tripped.

But, the devil takes that weakness and begins to come on you to keep that weakness in your body and make it worse. He wants to establish a spirit of infirmity that you can't shake off.

The spirit of infirmity tries to make your sickness into your identity – 'the blind man', 'the deaf woman', 'the cripple' – Satan loves those titles.

This is why, when I pray for the sick, I really view it as deliverance. I see all sickness like a snake seeking to poison us and suck the life out of us. Satan's plan for your life is to steal from you, kill you and destroy everything you have (John 10:10).

We see repeatedly in the scriptures that sickness is oppression of the devil:

> "...God anointed Jesus of Nazareth with the Holy Spirit and with power, who went about doing good and healing all who were oppressed by the devil, for God was with him."
> Acts 10:38

> "... The reason the Son of God appeared was to destroy the devil's work."
> 1 John 3:8

> "Jesus rebuked the demon, and it came out of the boy, and he was healed from that moment."
>
> Matthew 17:18

I do not mean that every sick person is possessed. But I do mean that all sickness has its roots in Satan and his minions. It is part of their attack on God's creation.

So what does Jesus come to do? He comes to free us from bondage. Back in the story in Luke 13:10, we see Jesus' response to the spirit of infirmity.

> "But when Jesus saw her, he called her to him and said to her, 'Woman, you are loosed from your infirmity.'"
>
> Luke 13:12

And we know that Jesus still wants to do that same thing today. He still wants to loose people from their infirmity because he is the same today as he was then.

> "Jesus Christ is the same yesterday, today, and forever."
>
> Hebrews 13:8

First, Jesus declared she was 'loosed' from her infirmity. But it goes on to tell us that Jesus then laid hands on her. Why, if she was already healed?

It seems Jesus dealt first with the 'spirit of infirmity' - the demon that had aggravated a physical illness. After dealing with that he laid hands on the woman and healed her physical symptoms. This shows us that sometimes people suffer from a spirit of infirmity in addition to a physical sickness or disease.

A prayer

I pray for those of you who are sick today – I curse every sickness and disease in your body. I bind the spirit of infirmity at work in your life. I break the power of sickness and disease attacking you today. I declare you are loosed from all sickness and disease. May the Holy Spirit come and touch your body right now. Sickness is going and healing is coming! Right now, in Jesus' name. Amen.

Chapter 5

Five things every believer should know about sickness

1. Sickness is a curse

When God was telling his people how to walk in blessing and avoid being under a curse, he said,

> "However, if you do not obey the LORD your God and do not carefully follow all his commands and decrees I am giving you today, all these curses will come upon you and overtake you."
>
> Deuteronomy 28:15

Then God listed the curses, which included sickness. Some people talk as though God sent the sickness to bless them with some profound insight. I think that is nonsense. God's word calls sickness a curse. Sickness is from Satan.

2. Sickness is bondage

> "The Lord answered him, 'You hypocrites! Doesn't each of you on the Sabbath untie his ox or donkey from the stall and lead it out to give it water? Then should not this woman, a

> daughter of Abraham, whom Satan has kept bound for eighteen long years, be set free on the Sabbath day from what bound her?'"
> Luke 13:15, 16

Jesus said the sickness was bondage to Satan. When we pray for people to be healed, we should approach it as a demonic spirit of sickness and disease.

3. Sickness is oppression from Satan

> "...how God anointed Jesus of Nazareth with the Holy Spirit and with power, who went about doing good and healing all who were oppressed by the devil, for God was with him."
> Acts 10:38

Sickness is used by Satan to oppress people. He tries to overwhelm them and to destroy them. He comes only to steal, kill and destroy.

4. Sickness is captivity

> "And the LORD turned the captivity of Job, when he prayed for his friends: also the LORD gave Job twice as much as he had before."
> Job 42:10 (KJV)

The Hebrew word '*sheb-ooth*' means captivity. Job was captive to sickness.

5. You have the right to be free!

"When evening came, many who were demon-possessed were brought to him, and he drove out the spirits with a word and healed all the sick. This was to fulfil what was spoken through the prophet Isaiah: 'He took up our infirmities and carried our diseases.'"
Matthew 8:16,17

Jesus took up your infirmities and sickness and every disease on the cross. Christians should never accept sickness. Our healing was purchased by Jesus, with his own blood, on the cross. His blood paid the price for our freedom. He bought us the right to be healed.

Chapter 6

The God who heals

In Exodus 15:26 God revealed himself as '*Jehovah rapha*' – literally 'I am [your] healer'.

Man's sin cut us off from God's blessing and subsequently led to sickness and death entering the world. Even so, God our Saviour was ready to redeem the situation. He comes to heal - to undo the work of Satan and man's folly. His healing touch is one of the benefits of a relationship with God.

"Bless the LORD, O my soul,
and forget not all His benefits:
who forgives all your iniquities,
who heals all your diseases,
who redeems your life from destruction,
who crowns you with loving kindness and tender mercies,
who satisfies your mouth with good things,
So that your youth is renewed like the eagle's."
Psalm 103:2-5

I love these words. First, he forgives all my wrongdoing. All. Second, he heals all my diseases. All. He redeems my life from destruction.

And the last line - he wants to restore my youth. Wouldn't you like to be a healthy teenager again? I would.

God's whole nature is to heal, restore, encourage and bless. That is his desire towards you. He doesn't come to put sickness on you to teach you a lesson - no! That is a lie of the devil. He comes to heal and restore.

Why doesn't God just heal everyone?

Why doesn't God just heal everyone all the time? That's a question I'm sometimes asked. If you reflect on God's nature and character for a while, you will realise that his greatest concern is for relationships – his relationship with you as an individual.

Increasingly, in the modern world we are treated like a number or just another customer or account holder. Personally I had a battle with a major bank, which went on for six months. The frustration of having to speak to a different person every time, and no one taking responsibility was crippling. Towards the end of the saga the 'Relationship Manager' got involved. I laughed at her title! She works 50 miles away from our bank, I have never met her or spoken to her though we've had the account for 15 years. So in what way was she ‘managing’ our ‘relationship’ with the bank?

By contrast, God knows us all personally, even the number of hairs on our head. His relationship with us is not computerised. The human spirit does not run under Windows. God doesn’t drop down a computer menu and select *‘Heal All’*. There is no relationship in that.

Obviously, God has prepared a kingdom after this life where there is no sickness, disease or death. But in order to get into that kingdom, we must be born again. That is, enter into a personal relationship with him.

Now, let me clarify. God does sometimes heal people who are not in a personal relationship with him. But his intervention is motivated by relationship.

For example, my friend Jacob grew up in India in a Hindu family and became literally sick to death. Here is his story in his own words.

> I was born in a strong Hindu traditional family in 1971. When I was 21 days old, my parents took me to the Hindu priest and named me after a Hindu god. On the same day my mother took a very hot needle and she burned my forehead and dedicated me to a Hindu

god. Every Friday, we used to worship 120 idols in our home.

In 1978, when I was 7 years old, I was dying with leukaemia. My parents spent all the money they had trying to get me cured. Eventually they joined me in the government hospital. After 48 days, the head doctor of the hospital came to my bed. After seeing all the medical reports, he said to my mother, 'Your son is going to die within two or three days. So you had better leave the hospital.'

So the doctor sent us away from the hospital. My parents took me to the bus station and we tried to go home. But by then we didn't have enough money for the journey home. So we only travelled halfway and stopped at a village where we have some relatives.

That night we heard the sound of some preachers at a Christian gospel meeting in the village. When my mother heard the sound of the gospel meeting she asked, 'Who is this they are speaking about? I've never heard this name, 'Jesus', before.'

My mother took me to the Christians' meeting. She was holding me wrapped in her sarong because I was too weak to walk. At the end of the meeting the Christians prayed for me. After the meeting my mother took me back home and laid me on my bed. She slept beside me because I was on my deathbed and about to die.

That night I was struggling to breathe. I laid my hands on my chest and I was breathing heavily. I felt I was about to die. I tried to speak, to tell my mother I was about to die but I could not speak. I was too weak even to open my mouth.

Then I saw a man come into the room. At first, I thought it was my father. The man came to my side and took my hand. He got me out of bed and we walked a little way. He sat on a rock and then asked me, 'Son, what is your name?'

I told him my name and told him that my parents gave me the name of a Hindu god. Then he laughed and said, 'Son, this is not your name.' Then he opened a book and showed me three letters in our language – Ja-Co-Bo. I read it to mean 'Jacob'.

Then he took a glass and poured something in to it and gave it to me to drink. I took the glass and I drank it. Then he laid his hand on my shoulder and he said, 'Son, you will not die. Go back.'

I turned from him to go back to my bed. As I did, I turned back to him and said, 'Sir, would you please tell me your name so I can tell my parents who you are?'

Then he looked me in the eyes and said, 'I am Jesus.'

The next thing I remember, I opened my eyes and my mother was sleeping at the side of my bed. I forgot about my blood cancer. I jumped up from my bed and began shouting, 'Mum! Mum! Jesus came to my bed! Jesus came to my bed!'

My parents woke up and were shocked that I could move. They thought I would die the very next moment. They said, 'What is happening to you? Are you dying?'

I said, 'Mum, no! I am not dying! Jesus came to my bed.' They began touching me, checking my temperature. They said, 'What has happened to you? You haven't walked for the last six months. You were just skin and bone but now you're walking like a healthy boy!'

Then I told them about how I met Jesus in the night. That very night, we all walked down to the Christian pastor's house. The pastor told us all about Jesus from the gospel of John. After he told us about Jesus, the three of us knelt down in front of the pastor. We told him we repented of our sin and we wanted to receive Jesus into our hearts. We went back home and told our relatives. But they were very angry and they rejected us from our caste.

In India we have a very strong caste system. They beat us up and punched us and excommunicated us from the caste for 12 years. All our relatives left us but Jesus never left our family.

Today, Jacob travels across India telling people about Jesus. In the early days, he would walk hundreds of miles, barefoot, to remote villages to tell people about the Jesus who came into his life.

He is often beaten for being a Christian but nothing stops him.

He is now the director of a thriving organisation that shows the love of Jesus through orphanages, leper colonies, and schools for poor children. His organisation has dug hundreds of wells across India to bring clean water to suffering people.

He has founded a Bible college and sends Indian missionaries across his homeland to tell of the God he found that night as a boy. Countless lives have been touched and saved physically and spiritually through the life of Jesus in this one man.

With hindsight, one can see that Jesus saw something in that dying Hindu boy that neither he nor his own family saw. Today, the most important thing in Jacob's life is his relationship with Jesus. You would always become aware of that within minutes of meeting him.

You see, the healing power of God is not some impersonal magic force channelled by some medium. No. The healing power of God is God himself, touching our spirit, restoring our soul and healing our body. That is why he revealed himself as '*Jehovah rapha*' – 'I am your healer'. That is why healing is coming now.

Chapter 7

The root of divine healing

Here's the deal. We can be healed because of something called 'the covenant'.

The dictionary describes a covenant as:

– a contract drawn up by deed.

– a clause in a contract.

– an agreement that brings about a relationship of commitment between God and his people.

We have covenants today. Marriage is a covenant, for example. The difference is that today's covenants are sometimes broken or ended. But God's covenant is for ever.

I want to look at what happened when God made this covenant with a human being. It began way back in the first book of the Bible.

> "Now the LORD had said to Abram: 'Get out of your country, from your family and from your father's house, to a land that I will show you. I will make you a great nation; I will bless you and make your name great; and you shall be a blessing. I will bless those who bless you, and I will curse him who curses

you; and in you all the families of the earth shall be blessed.'"

Genesis 12:1-3

The first thing we notice is that God told Abram to leave his father's house and leave the country. He was then living in what is modern-day Turkey. His father's family were involved in a pagan religion that worshipped the moon. (It is interesting that even today Turkey's flag shows a moon.)

God wanted Abram to get away from his family's false religion and come aside to a fresh relationship with himself.

To enter into the new covenant God has for us, we need to separate ourselves from false spirituality. We cannot mix new age healing with the healing of Jesus. God calls for spiritual purity.

Once Abram had obeyed God, God appeared to him again.

"After these things the word of the LORD came to Abram in a vision, saying, 'Do not be afraid, Abram. I am your shield, your exceedingly great reward.' But Abram said, 'Lord GOD, what will you give me, seeing I go childless, and the heir of my house is Eliezer of Damascus?' Then Abram said, 'Look, you have given me no offspring; indeed one born in my house is my heir!' And behold, the word of the LORD came to him, saying, 'This one shall not be your heir, but one who will come from your own body shall be your heir.' Then he brought him outside and said, 'Look now toward heaven, and count the stars if you are able to number them.' And he said to him, 'So shall your descendants be.' And he believed in the LORD, and he accounted it to him for righteousness."

Genesis 15:1-6

Secondly, we read that Abram and his wife were childless, yet God gives him a vision of the starry sky and tells him his descendants will be as numerous. The last sentence is important. 'Abram believed God'! That would not be an easy thing because what God was telling him was unbelievable. But he believed God. That is, he put his faith and trust in God's word. God always responds to faith. And we are told that God "accounted it to him for righteousness." Abram got some credit in his spiritual bank account by believing what God said in the face of contradicting circumstances.

"Then he said to him, 'I am the LORD, who brought you out of Ur of the Chaldeans, to give you this land to inherit it.' And he said,

> 'Lord GOD, how shall I know that I will inherit it?' So he said to him, 'Bring me a three-year-old heifer, a three-year-old female goat, a three-year-old ram, a turtledove, and a young pigeon.' Then he brought all these to him and cut them in two, down the middle, and placed each piece opposite the other; but he did not cut the birds in two. And when the vultures came down on the carcasses, Abram drove them away. Now when the sun was going down, a deep sleep fell upon Abram; and behold, horror and great darkness fell upon him."
>
> Genesis 15:7-12

Now when God promises Abram a land, Abram asks how can he know this is true? We could ask, 'How do I know God will heal me?' And God instructs him to bring several animals and cut them in two pieces. So what's going on here? Stick with me.

In his culture, the method of creating a covenant was familiar to Abram. For example, let's look at a hypothetical problem that may be solved by a covenant.

There are two families. The first family are farmers. They know how to grow crops. Their harvest is always bountiful. Unfortunately, thieves keep coming and attacking them and stealing their crops. This family are unable to defend themselves.

The second family are fighters. No one can overcome them. However, this family is useless at growing crops. They are often hungry.

Now in the culture of Abram at that time, these two families may come together to establish a covenant. All family members would have to attend. The elders of each family would agree the terms of the covenant. When all was agreed, they would take a cow or a goat and cut it in two and lay the pieces opposite each other. Then, with all the family watching, the elders of each family would join hands and walk in the blood and recite the terms of the covenant. Everything the farmers had now also belonged to the fighters. Everything the fighters had now also belonged to the farmers. From that moment, those two families became one family. Now the weaknesses in the families were cancelled out. The fighters would defend the farmers. And the farmers would feed the fighters. And this agreement could not be broken because it was agreed in blood.

So now picture Abram on that night when God told him to cut the animals in two and lay the pieces opposite. The ground would be covered in blood. Then Abram was amazed at what he saw.

> "And it came to pass, when the sun went down and it was dark, that behold, there appeared a smoking oven and a burning torch that passed between those pieces. On the same day the LORD made a covenant with Abram..."
>
> Genesis 15:17, 18

Abram saw the presence of the Living God 'walking' in the blood. God was saying effectively, 'Everything I have is yours and everything you have is mine.' So Abram, who became Abraham, received the covenant blessing from God.

So what does that blood-soaked ritual on a dark night in the Middle East have to do with us?

Well, when Jesus came, his purpose was to open this covenant blessing to all who would receive him. To remove the curse of sin and our fallen nature, and bring us under the blessing which Abraham received.

> "Christ has redeemed us from the curse of the law, having become a curse for us ... that the blessing of Abraham might come upon the

Gentiles in Christ Jesus..."

Galatians 3:13, 14

As Jesus bled and died on the cross, a new covenant was formed between God and man. Jesus was fully man and fully God. So when his blood ran down his crucified body, the blood of God and the blood of man mingled together in a new covenant.

Jesus foreshadowed this moment when he shared the Passover wine with his followers before his arrest.

"And he said to them, 'This is my blood of the new covenant, which is shed for many.'"

Mark 14:24

The very thought that God would say to us, 'All I have is yours' sounds incredible. Yet it is true. When Jesus taught about the kingdom of God, he implied as much. You may be familiar with the story of the prodigal son in Luke 15. The prodigal son represents those who are lost in sin. He returns and repents and is received back by his father. The father in the story represents God our heavenly Father. He throws a party for the penitent sinner. When the older brother hears the noise from the party, he becomes angry. He can't believe that this complete loser is being welcomed home like this. He accuses his father of never throwing even a small party for him. This older brother represents the believer - the one who is with the father and serving him. Now look at the words Jesus puts in the mouth of the father.

> "And he said to him, 'Son, you are always with me, and all that I have is yours.'"
> Luke 15:31

Two things: 1. You are always with me. 2. All I have is yours. That's a covenant statement right there.

So there is the offer of a divine exchange on the cross. All we have is God's. All he has is ours. So we give him our sin. He gives us his forgiveness. We give him our infirmity and our sickness. He gives us his healing. He takes our poverty and gives us his provision. He takes our fear. He gives us his peace.

From the moment he appeared to Abram on that dark night all those years ago, the plan was set to bring you into his covenant. His all is put at your disposal so the blessing of God can sweep across the earth.

I believe that on the cross, Jesus paid the full price for all sin, sickness and poverty. Every curse was lifted. Every oppressive demon was put on notice to quit. The power of Satan was crushed at last. All heaven was let loose.

Sickness is going. Healing is coming. Now!

Chapter 8

Say, don't pray

Clearly, Jesus taught his followers to pray.

> "And whatever things you ask in prayer, believing, you will receive."
> Matthew 21:22

He taught that we are to pray 'believing' which, if we are honest, often we don't. We just kind of hope some stuff will happen. In the Anglican Church we have weekly intercessions where we often mention the names of those who are sick. We say those odd words, 'Lord we pray for those who are sick...' and then list their names. I'm sure every week God bends his ear towards those prayers and asks, 'What do you pray for them?' Our prayer is so vague and unspecific it would be impossible to know if it was answered!

I can't help thinking we are just having an 'organ recital'. We mention hearts, livers, kidneys and lungs. We recite a list of organs but have no expectation that God will heal.

By contrast Jesus was always very specific. Often his 'prayer' was a command for sickness to go and healing to come.

> "Then, looking up to heaven, he sighed, and said to him, 'Ephphatha,' that is, 'Be opened.' Immediately his ears were opened, and the impediment of his tongue was loosed, and he spoke plainly."
>
> Mark 7:34, 35

Other times it seems more of a prophetic statement.

> "Then Jesus said to the centurion, 'Go your way; and as you have believed, so let it be done for you.' And his servant was healed that same hour."
>
> Matthew 8:13

Jesus also seems to put this power onto his followers. When you get the power, you are transformed from a follower to 'one who is sent' – or apostle, to use the Bible word.

There was a day when Jesus called the twelve disciples to him. He gives them power and then they are referred to as apostles.

> "And when he had called his twelve disciples to him, he gave them power over unclean spirits, to cast them out, and to heal all kinds of sickness and all kinds of disease. Now the names of the twelve apostles are these: ...These twelve Jesus sent out and command-

ed them, saying: '...as you go, preach, saying, 'The kingdom of heaven is at hand.' Heal the sick, cleanse the lepers, raise the dead, cast out demons. Freely you have received, freely give.'"

Matthew 10:1-8

What happened to change them from disciples (followers) to apostles (sent ones)? They got the power from Jesus.

Other times Jesus tells people to do something and then their healing comes as they obey him.

"Then he said to the man, 'Stretch out your hand.' And he stretched it out, and it was restored as whole as the other."

Matthew 12:13

At other times, perhaps the majority of times, Jesus responds to faith.

"Then Jesus answered and said to her, 'O woman, great is your faith! Let it be to you as you desire.' And her daughter was healed from that very hour."

Matthew 15:28

All this is different to how so many Christians pray for healing. Often it goes something like this: 'Lord we thank you for Dave and all he does for you. We thank you for his servant heart/

musical gift etc. We ask you to heal him today...'

It's almost like we are trying to convince God of the sick person's worthiness to be healed. But this is all wrong. Healing is on the basis of what Jesus did for lost sinners on the cross. It's based on a covenant made with the blood of Jesus. None of us are worthy - only Jesus.

Also in Mark 11:23,24 Jesus told us to 'speak to the mountain', not talk to him about the mountain! He said we will have whatever we say.

I am convinced we must speak directly to the sickness and treat it like the demon it is and command it to go in the name and authority of Jesus Christ.

Vaguely asking God to do something he has already told us to do rarely works.

When Jesus sent out the 72 in Luke 10:9 he told them to 'heal the sick'. He didn't say 'pray for the sick'. He'd given them power and authority and he expected them to do it. We have to rise up on the inside of us and take the authority Jesus gave us. We have to command the sickness to go, not start some vague prayer based on our own merits.

Chapter 9

Faith for healing

There are clearly two ways of getting healed through Christ. One is by faith - so often Jesus said to the cured, 'Your faith has made you well.' Here are a few references from Matthew's gospel where Jesus links healing to faith: 8:10, 9:2, 9:22, 9:29, 14:31, 15:28, 17:20, 21:21-46.

The second way to get healed is through the anointing. That is to find someone who has a powerful anointing on them and receive from them. I'm talking about the anointing of Jesus here, not spiritualists or New Age quacks.

In Luke 7:11 we read of a woman who did not come in faith and yet she received a wonderful miracle.

This story stands out, as this widow didn't come to Jesus with faith but was just attending her son's funeral in grief. She'd already lost her husband and now her son had died. I do not believe this woman had any faith whatsoever.

I know from personal experience what it is to attend your own son's funeral. It's an experience that feels so wrong – a deeper grief.

She didn't come with faith but Jesus got her attention with an unexpected miracle. I think God does that sometimes. He gets people's attention with something they weren't expecting.

Secondly, the story speaks of two large crowds. The first crowd was with Jesus.

> "Now it happened, the day after, that he went into a city called Nain; and many of his disciples went with him, and a large crowd."
> Luke 7:11

Why was this crowd with him? They had seen the miracles, heard the life-giving teaching – they were a happy crowd. They may even have been singing, though we are not told if they were or not.

The second large crowd was with the widow.

> "And when he came near the gate of the city, behold, a dead man was being carried out, the only son of his mother; and she was a widow. And a large crowd from the city was with her."
> Luke 7:12

This crowd was not happy. This was a crowd in grief and mourning. They were on their way to a funeral to bury the dead.

The story tells us that Jesus was going into Nain and that the funeral was coming out of

Nain. The two crowds clashed. Joy met grief.

Then it says something happened in the clash.

> "When the Lord saw her, he had compassion on her and said to her, 'Do not weep.'"
> Luke 7:13

There comes a moment in our life when heaven beckons. It's a defining moment. Oh the grace and mercy of our God!

As I think about this story, I realise I am surrounded by dead people every day. Oh they look alive. They walk around, they talk, they eat, they watch TV, they laugh and cry and do all the things I do. But inside they are dead. They had a dream for their life, but it didn't happen. They lost hope. They let their dream die.

Let me ask you a question. Are your memories bigger than your dreams? The memories of past hurt and disappointments, of dashed hopes and rejections, of abuse? Are those memories bigger than your dreams?

I would love to have been in Nain that day. Something different happened.

Normally, when we see a funeral, we observe it in quiet respect and stand aside for the procession to pass.

But Jesus did something profoundly different. He stepped into the road and stopped the funeral.

> "Then he came and touched the open coffin, and those who carried him stood still. And he said, 'Young man, I say to you, arise.'"
> Luke 7:14

Today, Jesus interrupts the burial of your dreams. He steps into the procession of the funeral of your hopes and dreams. And he says to you, 'Young man, young woman, I say to you, arise.'

Rise up! It's not too late! It's not over till the barren woman sings (Isaiah 54:1)!

That dream that God put in your heart may be the reason you were born. Today Jesus is doing the unexpected and giving you a fresh start beyond your imagining. It is time for you to play your part. To rise up!

> "Then fear came upon all, and they glorified God, saying, 'A great prophet has risen up among us;' and, 'God has visited his people.'"
> Luke 7:16

'God has visited his people!' What a wonderful phrase. Isn't that what we want? Maybe today God is going to visit you!

But for this woman, she received the physical miracle of her dead son returned to life! And she got that without faith. Clearly God responds to faith and also does some kingdom stuff to people without faith.

It seems to me that it's about community. If we are people in the community of faith, God expects faith in us and responds to that. But for the lost, without faith, God moves in the anointing. And we may wonder why he doesn't just heal everyone, but Jesus described the anointing of the Holy Spirit like this:

> "The wind blows where it wishes, and you hear the sound of it, but cannot tell where it comes from and where it goes. So is everyone who is born of the Spirit."
>
> John 3:8

The final chapter of life, in heaven, is where all sickness is finally eliminated. God only tarries so that more people may enter the kingdom and be saved. In the meantime, the kingdom of God breaks through into the kingdom of this world through faith and through the anointing of God. The purpose of the anointing is to break the yoke of slavery that Satan puts on us.

> "...the yoke will be destroyed because of the anointing..."
>
> Isaiah 10:27

Centuries back, the Roman Catholic Church sold 'indulgences'. Basically, people could pay the Church some money to buy forgiveness for their sins. The practice was also extended to selling indulgences so that dead relatives could escape punishment. Any thinking Christian today would be opposed to such an idea. But with the increase of Christian television we are seeing something similar. Don't get me wrong, I am not against Christian TV. I have appeared on the GOD channel myself! There are some excellent ministries out there. But there are some that are suspect. There are different shades of the practice but it basically amounts to the idea of 'Send us 100 dollars today and your healing will come as a result.'

I think that is very like the sale of indulgences. I have often ministered in Africa, in poor areas where people have nothing. Often we see a higher proportion of healings in those areas. At those times I really get moved by God's blessing on the poor. So clearly, you don't have to pay for healing, otherwise these people could never get healed.

Now, it is true that those with finance should give generously to the work of the kingdom. Our ministry at RSVP Trust only happens because of many generous supporters. But, and it's a big but, you don't need to send me money, buy my book or get some special water or other gizmo to get healed. Actually, you don't even need to meet me! God can heal you right now wherever you are.

I do know that God leads us to do some unusual things in the healing ministry sometimes.

> "Now God worked unusual miracles by the hands of Paul, so that even handkerchiefs or aprons were brought from his body to the sick, and the diseases left them and the evil spirits went out of them."
> Acts 19:11, 12

It's just that when someone connects the expectation of paying for something with healing, I think they have wandered into manipulation or exploitation.

I believe in giving to Christian ministries. I love to give. My wife and I give personally and our ministry at RSVP Trust sends thousands of pounds every month to bring hope and help to some of the poorest people on earth.

It is very good to give. But your healing is not dependent on it in the sense that if you don't pay, we won't pray.

Jesus preached the Sermon on the Mount. Some modern preachers seem to preach the Sermon on the Amount. Don't get me wrong, I believe God's plan for us is prosperity and health.

> "Beloved, I pray that you may prosper in all things and be in health, just as your soul prospers."
>
> 3 John 2

Now when the anointing is not available, I believe we can stir our faith and increase it by following God's instruction. My previous book - *A Word about your Healing* - goes into more detail about building up your faith for healing. But here are a few pointers.

As I said in chapter 2, the Bible tells us that each of us has a measure of faith:

> "...God has dealt to each one a measure of faith."
>
> Romans 12:3

That faith, which everyone has, can be increased. It grows when we hear God's word.

> "So then faith comes by hearing, and hearing by the word of God."
>
> Romans 10:17

I remember years ago a deaf lady got cross with me when I preached on those words. 'If faith comes by hearing,' she said, 'then I cannot get faith because I cannot hear!'

Sometimes those of us who can hear sounds don't really 'hear' what people are saying because we're not listening. We can 'hear' the word of God as much by reading as by listening. The question is, are we 'receiving' God's word into our heart? Are we meditating on it and believing it? That is how faith comes.

And it needs to be a regular practice. Faith doesn't come by having heard (past tense) but by hearing (present tense).

We can listen to and read teaching on his word. One of the things people say about my little book - *A Word about your Healing* - is that they had never before seen some of the scriptures I quoted. When they saw them, faith came and, in many cases, healing came.

I also have a podcast for the same reason, so the word of faith can go out into all the earth. I was greatly encouraged last year when I got an email from a man in Australia telling me a small group from his church listen to my podcast. I've never been to Australia yet the word of God is reaching that far-away place and faith is increasing because of it.

Sometimes people want a list of steps to healing, or to know what 'the rules' are. Human beings always want a law for things, even though history tells us we will always break the law anyway. If there is a rule to healing, it's that it normally works by faith. That is, we hear God's word, believe it and receive it and then faith produces a miracle.

> "Therefore he who supplies the Spirit to you and works miracles among you, does he do it by the works of the law or by the hearing of faith?"
>
> Galatians 3:5

We need to spend time hearing from God and the best way to do that is to slowly and thoughtfully read his word in the Bible. As we do that, we may hear the word God is speaking to us personally, right now.

Chapter 10
Dare to pray

When I mention healing in Christian circles I often feel like I'm swimming against the current. So many Christians and many leaders are fearful of praying for healing.

'What if it doesn't work?' This is the vexing question that paralyses well–intentioned Christians the world over. 'What if I pray and nothing happens?'

> "He who observes the wind will not sow, and he who regards the clouds will not reap."
> Ecclesiastes 11:4

'What if it doesn't work?' is a question rooted in fear. You may as well ask, 'What if I walked past a tall building and someone pushed a piano out of the window and it fell on me?' It is very unlikely. One thing I can virtually guarantee is that something will happen when you pray for healing. The Bible says that 'nothing' is impossible with God. If 'nothing' is impossible, then 'something' has to happen!

We could ask, 'What if I preach the gospel and no one gets saved?' Or 'What if we share communion and nothing happens?' If God has commanded us to do certain things, don't you think we should do them and leave the outcome to him?

Jesus gives his followers power to heal the sick.

> "And when He had called his twelve disciples to him, he gave them power over unclean spirits, to cast them out, and to heal all kinds of sickness and all kinds of disease."
> Matthew 10:1

He didn't even say we should pray but that we should heal the sick.

> "Heal the sick, cleanse the lepers, raise the dead, cast out demons. Freely you have received, freely give."
> Matthew 10:8

Just as you don't criticise a child's faltering steps when he is learning to walk, neither does God chastise us when we try to walk in faith. He is there to teach us and encourage us.

I think the best lesson I learned about healing was that... it's not me. It's not about me cranking up my faith or whipping up a crowd. It is the love of God touching human hearts and bodies.

After all these years I am still amazed at how God heals and what he does. I remember years ago in Uganda we were praying for the sick. Two children were brought forward, a boy and a girl, both about 9 years old. Both were deaf and mute. We laid hands on the little girl first. As we were praying for her, the little boy started hearing and speaking. I thought, 'God! We are over here not over there!'

> "The wind blows where it wishes, and you hear the sound of it, but cannot tell where it comes from and where it goes. So is everyone who is born of the Spirit."
>
> John 3:8

For years I knew we had a command to pray for the sick and for years I did. Very few remarkable miracles happened. I knew the problem was not with God, so I kept praying. I prayed so long with so few results that I got to the place where I wasn't expecting much to happen.

Then one day, something happened! I was with my friend Adam out in Rwanda. I was speaking at a conference and on the last day we offered to pray for the sick. About 100 of the 500 people who were there came forward. We prayed for everyone all at once. As we were coming to the end of the prayer time, a lady began shouting in the crowd. She pointed at me, shouting in her own language. The interpreter began to smile and told me, 'She is saying that she has been listening to you preach and she didn't know you were a 'mzungu' (white person) because she has been blind for 12 years. But as we were praying, her eyes opened and now she can see your face!'

As she was telling her story another, younger lady came to tell us that she too had been blind for 12 years and she too could now see.

Another lady began touching her toes to demonstrate that her chronic abdominal pains had disappeared. And so it went on, as all heaven was let loose in that meeting.

Something happened that day. First, people who were blind could suddenly see. Second, we had done nothing different that day to any other day. Once you have seen the power of God heal in such a dramatic way, you know there is no reason why anyone could not be healed.

It's not you, it's God.

A year later I was in Rwanda again. I was to go up-country to speak to 30 Anglican clergymen. When we reached the place, word had got around and 1,200 people had gathered outside the church. Some had walked 25 miles to be there. We decided to hold the conference outside the church with everyone.

Every night I prayed for the sick. On the third night, I felt God tell me to ask the crowd if any had been healed. I was reluctant. I hadn't 'felt' anything when I prayed for them and didn't think anything had happened.

However, when I asked the crowd if anyone had been healed, almost half the crowd raised their hands. For about half an hour we heard story after story of people who had been healed on the previous nights.

As we were listening to each tell their story, I noticed a man at the back of the crowd dancing and leaping from one foot to the other. Finally I asked, 'What is that man doing?'

He told us how he had been crippled and was unable to walk. Four friends had carried him to the meeting. When we prayed on the first night, strength had returned to his legs and he could now walk... and dance! Sound familiar?

My message to all Christians and leaders especially, is to pray, keep praying and never be discouraged. I can't tell you what will happen but I know something will happen. PUSH - Pray Until Something Happens.

One example, earlier this year I was speaking in Chorleywood at a healing meeting. I prayed for many people. A young man wrote to me after the meeting. He told me he had come with a very painful shoulder. When I prayed nothing happened. He bought my book - *A Word about your Healing*. He read it and the following week he was asked to pray with someone with a very painful shoulder. As soon as he began to pray, the man he was praying with was healed. He said it had given him great encouragement that he too would get healing for his shoulder!

So dare to pray. Don't 'observe the wind' or 'regard the clouds', otherwise you will not sow or reap the healing miracles.

Remember - sickness is going. Healing is coming. Now!

Chapter 11

Healing the body

God wants you to be whole. You may be reading this book because you have a physical sickness. I believe God wants to you to be completely healed of that sickness. However, I think God wants to do even more. He is concerned with your whole being - body, soul and spirit.

An example of this is in Acts chapter 3 when Peter and John go up to the temple to pray. On the way they meet a lame beggar who asks for money. Peter replies that they don't have money but they have the anointing. The man is healed, and Luke's description of what happens is interesting.

> "So he, leaping up, stood and walked and entered the temple with them – walking, leaping, and praising God."
>
> Acts 3:8

First, it says he walked - so he was healed physically. Then he leaped, which means he got emotional - his soul was healed. Finally, he praised God - his spirit was healed. So we see that God was interested in far more than just healing his legs. He wanted to restore his relationship with his heavenly Father.

So in the next 3 chapters I want to look at the different types of healing.

While you're waiting for physical healing

I've seen many people healed from many things. Just a couple of weeks ago a doctor got healed of arthritis in his knees after I prayed for healing in a church service. Last year a blind lady was leaving the church after a healing meeting and thought she saw someone's face as she left. She didn't believe it at first, but by Wednesday of that week her eyesight was restored.

These are great stories… but what should we do when we are praying for our own healing and it hasn't yet appeared? Here are a few thoughts for those who are praying and waiting for healing to manifest in their own bodies.

We need to view sickness like a snake climbing up our leg. If that happened we wouldn't just mildly complain about it to others. No. We'd stand up, shake it off our leg and probably shout a bit! We may even curse it and then beat it till it was dead.

When we're trying to get healed of a long-standing illness, I think there are a few things we should know. If the sickness came as a long process of decline, let's not be surprised if our healing is a gradual process of improvement as well.

Think of the great oil tankers out at sea. You can't just turn those things round. When the captain turns the wheel, nothing seems to happen for a while. But if he's consistent, if he keeps the wheel turned in the same direction, gradually the vessel will turn. He mustn't give up; he must be consistent.

When we are waiting for healing, we, too, must be consistent in our faith – looking to God as the source of our healing, trusting and believing that he wants to heal, will heal and has healed.

It's a bit like your sin:

– you *were* forgiven (on the cross)

– you *are* forgiven (as you receive the gift)

– you *will be* forgiven (at the judgement)

Our healing really took place on the cross 2000 years ago. Now we are enforcing that healing through declaring what God has said and agreeing with it.

> "... if two of you agree on earth concerning anything that they ask, it will be done for them by my Father in heaven."
> Matthew 18:19

We begin by speaking out our faith - we say what we want, not what we have. So we begin to say 'I'm healed' instead of going around telling everyone we're ill. It's an act of faith.

For example, Joel 3:10 says, "Let the weak say, 'I am strong.'" Why would the Bible tell us to do that?

We do this strange thing because Jesus said, "...he will have whatever he says" (Mark 11:23). So we speak the solution, not the problem.

So, for example, as I am praying for my friend Tracy who has cancer, I am saying, 'Tracy is healed. The name of Jesus is above every name. It's above the name of cancer. I command this cancer to leave now. I declare that it's the cancer that will curl up and die - not Tracy. Tracy is healed by the wounds of Jesus. Cancer is going NOW! Healing is coming NOW!' And I should pray like that every day - as long as it takes.

We should be expectant. We should tell Satan that his plan, to steal, kill and destroy (John 10:10), will not work in our body because our healing has been purchased with the blood of Jesus.

We need to come to the place where we have as much confidence that we are healed as we have that we are forgiven. How do you know your sin is forgiven? Can you prove it? No. You are trusting that the blood of Jesus paid the price on the cross, that it's a done deal in the Spirit and that you have passed from death to life. Gradually an inner witness grows in your spirit.

Well it's the same covenant that heals us as forgives us. How do we know we are healed? It begins by trusting that the blood of Jesus paid the price for our healing. (Matthew 8:17 'He took our infirmities'.) We believe it's a done deal - we don't need to qualify it with little get-out clauses for God (just as we wouldn't do that for forgiveness). Gradually an inner witness grows that we are in possession of our healing. When we get it in the spirit, shortly after it will manifest in the flesh.

Like Jesus said to Jairus, when the servant said 'your child is dead, trouble the master no more', he replied 'only believe' – and keep believing and don't quit believing.

I love Psalm 103 because I did some research and found that the Hebrew word translated here as 'all' actually means... ALL!

"Bless the LORD, O my soul,
and forget not all his benefits:
who forgives all your iniquities,
who heals all your diseases,

who redeems your life from destruction,
who crowns you with lovingkindness and tender mercies,
who satisfies your mouth with good things,
so that your youth is renewed like the eagle's."

Psalm 103:2-5

I'm over 50 years old but I declare with the psalmist, 'My youth is being renewed like the eagle's.'

Whatever you are facing today, you need to stand up on the inside, like David running to face Goliath in battle, boldly confident that you are facing a defeated enemy. You are healed in the name of Jesus!

Chapter 12

Healing the heart

> "Keep your heart with all diligence,
> for out of it spring the issues of life."
> Proverbs 4:23

The Bible tells us to 'keep' or to 'guard' our heart with all diligence. To 'guard' means: to watch over in order to control entry and exit, to take precautions against, to protect against damage or harm. The dictionary describes diligence as 'careful and persistent work or effort'. In other words, we must be extremely careful about our heart. I'm not talking about the lump of flesh that pumps blood around our body, though naturally we are all keen to protect that. I'm talking about the heart as the centre of our thoughts and emotions. We talk of having 'peace in our heart' or of being 'hard-hearted'.

The Bible says we must strive to protect this place because out of it spring the issues of life. It's the place where we love or hate. It's a strong force in our decision-making and so influential in our actions.

It is also the place where we get wounded from time to time. Harsh words or a bad experience can get to our heart. We have to decide to get better or get bitter. When we are growing up, it's easy to get hurt by the words or actions of others. If love was withheld from us in our formative years, or we encountered periods of bullying and control by others, our heart can be wounded. Sadly, that is just life and true for most of us to one degree or another.

> "For I am poor and needy, and my heart is wounded within me."
> Psalm 109:22 (NIV)

God can heal you everywhere you hurt. One of my favourite speakers is Joyce Meyer. Joyce was sexually abused by her father, when she was young, and grew up with a broken heart. Yet today she seems so free - she has even managed to restore her relationship with her father, with God's help. She gives me hope for myself and everyone else because, if God could heal Joyce's heart, he can do it for you and me too.

I've met many broken-hearted people who have been deeply wounded in their heart. These hurts can hold people captive for years - in some cases for a lifetime. So we must get healing for our heart and keep it.

In 1987 our son died just a short time after both my parents died prematurely. He was almost three years old. It was a crushing experience that deeply wounded my heart. But I sought the Lord for healing of my heart. Naturally we have to grieve when a loved one dies - that is a healthy thing to do. But sometimes, when we are grieving, the devil comes and tries to put on us a spirit of grief, which is not healthy. His plan is to trap us in constant sadness.

A little counselling may help when our heart is wounded - I'm not against that - but true healing of the heart can only come from God. Sometimes, in counselling, we go round and round the problem and don't resolve it. We don't realise that God is closer than we think.

> "The LORD is close to the broken-hearted and saves those who are crushed in spirit."
> Psalm 34:18 (NIV)

My experience was that my heart became very hard. I was so hurt I could not feel any more. My heart was like stone. But as I sought the Lord, I had an experience of my hard heart being removed and a new heart being put in me. What happened to me is best expressed by the words of the prophet Ezekiel.

> "I will give you a new heart and put a new spirit in you; I will remove from you your heart of stone and give you a heart of flesh."
> Ezekiel 36:26 (NIV)

Being burdened with a heavy heart, with thoughts that turn over and over in our mind, is very unpleasant. Endlessly rehearsing, in our mind, every possible scenario and outcome is exhausting. This is nothing new. The Psalmist wrote about this thousands of years ago.

> "How long must I wrestle with my thoughts and every day have sorrow in my heart? How long will my enemy triumph over me?"
> Psalm 13:2 (NIV)

We need to deal with the issues of our heart, otherwise they will deal with us. They will fester and grow even darker. Every murder began with a resentment, which grew into a hatred, which gave birth to a killing. This is why we must guard our heart with all diligence.

> "For out of the heart come evil thoughts, murder, adultery, sexual immorality, theft, false testimony, slander."
> Matthew 15:19 (NIV)

In order to stop these evil things coming out of our heart, we must put good things into our heart. We do this by reading, meditating on and thinking about God's word. Memorising scripture stores it up in our hearts and brings light into our inner darkness.

"The precepts of the LORD are right, giving

joy to the heart. The commands of the LORD are radiant, giving light to the eyes."
Psalm 19:8 (NIV)

The trick is to really focus on God and worship him and love him first and above all things. When trouble or anguish comes begin to praise and worship God. He already knows your troubles, so don't keep repeating them to him. But find a song or prayer of worship and sing it out to him. When you need a breakthrough, P.U.S.H - Praise Until Something Happens.

Some friends wrote the following words on our wedding card. After more than 30 years of marriage, we have found them to be true.

"Delight yourself in the LORD and he will give you the desires of your heart."
Psalm 37:4 (NIV)

If we are going to guard our heart, remember God's word tells us we must do it 'with all diligence' or with 'careful and persistent work or effort'. This is so important we should allocate a space every day to check our heart. I find it works best by spending a little time alone first thing in the day and last thing at night. It's not always possible but it should be our default routine. The Bible has a simple prayer for these moments.

"Create in me a pure heart, O God, and renew a steadfast spirit within me."
Psalm 51:10 (NIV)

Healing for our heart begins with sorting out our relationships. To have peace in our heart requires peace in our relationships, as far as it depends on us. If our relationships are chaotic, it will be hard to keep peace in our heart. Part of our ministry at RSVP Trust is with people involved in addiction to drugs and those involved in the sex industry. Their lives are often chaotic because they often live without boundaries. Even though we – our team – all have issues, confusion and emotional baggage to a certain degree, just bringing our bit of stability to the relationship with these people can be a great blessing. We're far from perfect but most of us have sorted out some boundaries for our relationships.

Relationships will always be your greatest source of pain and your greatest source of joy. We were created for relationships. When they are good they are such a blessing. When they go wrong, they are so painful. But this is life.

Above all, healing for our heart begins with sorting out our relationship with God. Opening our heart to him and allowing him access to our inmost thoughts is the beginning of healing for our heart.

> "Search me, O God, and know my heart; test me and know my anxious thoughts."
> Psalm 139:23 (NIV)

Some people want to serve God but only as advisers. If we want real healing in our heart, we must give everything over to God. We must let him determine the outcome of situations. We must grasp, in spite of all our self-centred, arrogant thinking, that God knows far better than we do how to act in every situation.

> "Trust in the LORD with all your heart and lean not on your own understanding; in all your ways acknowledge him, and he will make your paths straight."
> Proverbs 3:5,6 (NIV)

One thing that will darken your heart very quickly is unforgiveness. If we are holding forgiveness from someone, it will poison our heart.

Forgiving someone does not mean allowing them to repeat the offence. I remember a lady who struggled to accept she should forgive her abusive ex-husband because she thought it would mean going back to him and subjecting herself to further abuse. No, that's not what forgiveness means. We can forgive someone whilst also giving them a boundary that what they did must not happen again. Or, perhaps more realistically, we give ourselves a boundary that we will not let it happen again. It may mean cutting off an abusive relationship.

By the way… if your spouse or partner is hitting you or being violent, you need to leave. And you need to leave now.

Once you are free, you need to let go of the past because, if you don't, the one who hurt you is still controlling you and poisoning your heart and robbing you of your peace.

When I get hurt and find it difficult to forgive the other person, I remember something my friend Noel once said. Noel was violently raped by a priest when he was 12 years old. I have written about it in Noel's book but it was so violent and evil I don't want to mention the details here. The abuse went on for three years and robbed him of his youth. When I asked him how he could possibly forgive this unrepentant priest who went on to abuse a lot of young boys, Noel's words shocked me. 'What if God acted like that towards us? What if he was so hurt about what we did to his Son that he refused to forgive us? We'd all be going to hell. If God forgave us for what we have done, we must forgive others like he told us to. Forgiving my abuser has set me free. It enabled me to replace his lies with the truth.'

Forgiveness is healing. Forgiveness is diligently guarding your heart. It is guarding what goes in and out of it, making sure only the good things come in and out.

Sometimes I think we spend far too long looking at where we've been and where we are. When what we should be looking at is where we are going. What I am sure of is that our heart is very precious and will determine our future happiness. This is why Christians sometimes use the phrase 'I invited Jesus into my heart'. What does that mean? It means that we allow Jesus to deal with all our pain, all our hurt, all our frustration and invite him to live in that secret place.

The alternative is that our heart becomes filled with dark thoughts, strife and anger. And 'anger' is only one letter away from 'danger'.

Even if we get our body and our heart healed, we still have a greater, much more urgent need of healing that most of us are unaware of – the healing of our soul.

We have already looked at the importance of what words come out of our mouth. We need to understand that what is in our heart will come out of our mouth.

> "For out of the abundance of the heart the mouth speaks."
> Matthew 12:34

These are the two places we need to have the word of God. If we put his word in our heart, it will come out of our mouth and that is a powerful moment.

> "But what does it say? 'The word is near you, in your mouth and in your heart' (that is, the word of faith which we preach)."
>
> Romans 10:8

Chapter 13
Healing the soul

I want to talk in this chapter about the most important healing we all need. A cure for what has been called the 'sin-sick soul'. Whatever you do, don't skip over this chapter because this is the most important part of this book.

Men and women became separated from their Creator and live lives ill at ease or in dis-ease as a result. The root cause of all sickness is our separation from God. Though God has reconciled the world through Jesus and Satan is defeated, still Satan comes at us with sickness and disease (2 Corinthians 5:18).

When Satan puts sickness on us it can be a battle, sometimes to the death, to get rid of it. The trump card of Jesus though, is that he overcame death. So even if our sickness were to end in death, if we know and love Jesus Christ, it doesn't end in death at all. It restarts in an imperishable new life. But this blessing is not automatic. It can only be gained through a relationship with Jesus – a relationship of obedience to him.

Jesus came into the world to bring complete restoration to every human being who submits to his authority.

Richard Roberts put it this way:

'Jesus came to take off you what the devil put on;
to take out of you what the devil put in;
to put back in what the devil took out;
to put back on you what the devil took off.'

I like that because it speaks of that spirit of 'steal, kill and destroy' (John 10:10) that is the cause of our ills, and also speaks of the glorious restoration of Jesus.

The first time I read the four gospels, I was actually looking for contradictions. I was reading as a sceptic. I was sure that Jesus was dead and buried and that most of his recorded life was a fairy story.

But as I read his words something changed. There is something unique about the words of Jesus – they are living words (Hebrews 4:12). So as we look at how to get healing for our soul or more accurately our spirit, I want to look at a few things Jesus said on the matter.

Jesus taught people about an alternative kingdom. He ministered during the Roman occupation of Israel. The mighty Roman Empire seemed, at that time, invincible. Yet somehow, this humble travelling, miracle-working rabbi suggested there was a more powerful kingdom and anyone who wanted to could enter into that kingdom if they followed his teaching.

It seemed the price for entry into that kingdom was unaffordable yet he said he would pay the price for entry. So that just leaves the matter of whether we will enter or not.

He painted various pictures about how we could get into this wonderful kingdom and, the price for entry having been paid, it now remains with us to enter or not. He also taught that there would be hell to pay later on if we didn't enter. It was like a man seeing a fire in a large building, sounding the alarm and pointing to the fire exit. Yet while some went for the exit, others tried to go their own way and perished.

That may sound far-fetched but at around 7:30pm on 18 November 1987, a fire broke out at King's Cross underground station in London. The station and tunnels filled with fire and smoke. I remember watching a news report at the time and hearing that a policeman saw people still going down into the station and so he spread wide his arms and warned them, to try and stop them perishing. Several people ignored him and ran headlong to their death. 31 people died that day, even though someone in authority warned them and was there to save them.

Jesus opened wide his arms for us on the cross. He calls to us to be saved from the fire ahead by turning to him. Some respond and some ignore him. Those who ignore him will perish despite his love, his sacrifice and his word being available to them. If we want to go to heaven we must go via King's Cross. We must go his way. When asked the way to heaven, Jesus said, "I am the Way... No one comes to the Father but by me" (John 14:6).

Jesus taught that it takes action on our part to enter into this kingdom where sickness is banished. We may have to swim against the current of this world and its thinking.

> "Enter through the narrow gate. For wide is the gate and broad is the road that leads to destruction, and many enter through it. But small is the gate and narrow the road that leads to life, and only a few find it."
> Matthew 7:13, 14 (NIV)

These are profound words. The entry into his kingdom is not through anything glaring, brash, loud or obvious. Nor through the way that most people live their lives. It's through a narrow gate, a small gate and only a few find it.

In John's gospel, chapter 3, Jesus uses a different picture. He told an old man that he must be 'born again'. The old man didn't understand how he could go into his mother's womb again. But Jesus said he was speaking spiritually.

He means that we have to be born into God's kingdom. When I was born, I was born into the United Kingdom and am therefore a citizen of that country.

So how can a person be born again, a second time? In John's gospel chapter 1, we read that when Jesus went to his own people – the Jewish nation – his own people rejected him – at least the vast majority anyway. But then John, one of Jesus' inner circle, says that if we 'receive' him we get power to become God's child.

> "He came to his own, and his own did not receive him. But as many as received him, to them he gave the right to become children of God, to those who believe in his name: who were born, not of blood, nor of the will of the flesh, nor of the will of man, but of God."
> John 1:11-13

The word translated 'right' is perhaps more accurately translated 'power' or 'authority' in this context, from the Greek word '*exousia*'.

So we become born again children of God by 'receiving' Jesus.

When we connect with people through social networking sites like Facebook, we have to click 'accept friend request'. When we do, we are warned that accepting this friend will give them access to all our information. To receive Jesus is to give him access and in this case, authority over all our life. It is to submit ourselves to his authority, to his way of doing and being right. It doesn't mean we'll never go wrong again but if we do, we can quickly turn from what we know is wrong and put right anything that is wrong as far as it depends on us.

So how do we 'receive' Jesus? The Bible says his own people rejected him. So it is firstly to not reject him. I may give you a Christmas gift, all nicely wrapped. But you haven't 'received' it until you take hold of it, unwrap it and use it.

All that is wrong with our lives, Jesus forgives when we turn to him. He can forgive us because he paid the price for our forgiveness with his own blood when he was executed on a Roman cross. There was a divine exchange. He took our sin and offers us forgiveness. He took our sicknesses and bore our infirmities and offers us healing. He took our death and offers us life.

"Bless the LORD, O my soul,
and forget not all his benefits:
who forgives all your iniquities,
who heals all your diseases,
who redeems your life from destruction,
who crowns you with lovingkindness and tender mercies,
who satisfies your mouth with good things,
so that your youth is renewed like the eagle's."

Psalms 103:2-5

So we must receive Jesus – take him for ourselves, 'unwrap' his gift and make him the focus of our life.

Jesus gave his friend John a message for several churches when he appeared to him on the island of Patmos. These people thought they were fine but Jesus said they were not. Their main fault was they had shut Jesus out of their lives. They hadn't fully received him. This is what he said to them.

"Here I am! I stand at the door and knock. If anyone hears my voice and opens the door, I will come in and eat with him, and he with me."

Revelation 3:20 (NIV)

He was saying that he was shut outside of

their life. They had not received him. But in the picture he uses, he said he was ‘knocking at their door’ and that if they opened the door, he would come in and be with them and ‘eat’ with them. In other words, come into a close relationship with them.

So where is Jesus in relation to you? Is he in your life, in your heart? Or is he outside? If he is outside, and you are reading this, these words are his ‘knocks’ at your door. Will you open your heart and let him come in? Or will you reject him and keep him out of your life? Jesus said:

> “Whoever confesses me before men, him I will also confess before my Father who is in heaven. But whoever denies me before men, him I will also deny before my Father who is in heaven.”
>
> Matthew 10:32, 33

Will you receive Jesus today? He loves you and is calling to you now.

If you are ready to receive him, to commit the rest of your life to him, here is a prayer to pray. Imagine Jesus standing before you. Don’t worry that you don’t feel good enough - he will receive you just as you are. Speak out these words to Jesus and he will come into your life.

Lord Jesus,
I want to know you today.
Please forgive me for the past.
For all the things I wish I hadn't done.
For all the good things I wish I had done but didn't do.
(Take a moment to mention specific things...)

I believe you gave your life on the cross for me.
I now give my life to you.
Come into my life today.
Come in as my Saviour to give me life.
Come in as my Lord to guide me.
Come in as my Friend to be with me.

Fill me with your Holy Spirit and give me a new life.
And I will serve you for the rest of my life.
Amen.

What now?

If you have said this prayer of commitment and meant it, Jesus has come into your life. In order to maintain this new life, there are a few things you need to do.

You have entered into a new relationship with

Jesus. Any relationship that is starved of conversation will grow cold and die. So you need to talk with Jesus every day.

The best way to do this is to read some of his words in the Bible (preferably in a modern translation – The Message or The New International Version are good ones). You'll find the words of Jesus about two-thirds of the way through the Bible in the books of Matthew, Mark, Luke and John. (Use the contents page if you can't find them!)

After reading some of his words, talk to him and ask him to be involved in your day. Many people find first thing in the morning a good time for this, so they take God into the day with them.

In coming into this new relationship with Jesus, you have also come into a new relationship with God's family. So find a church where you can grow in your new relationship and where you can learn more of Jesus, and make new friends. Church should be a friendly and exciting place to be.

Many churches today have house groups or home groups – a few people meet together during the week in someone's home to look at the Bible and learn together. Speak to the leader of the church about joining one of these.

It's also important not to be shy about what you have done. Tell someone what you have done today. Start with someone you think will be pleased to hear. Never apologise for being a Christian.

Chapter 14

Keeping your healing

In John 10:10 Jesus tells us that Satan is a thief who comes to steal, kill and destroy. Many people have prayed the prayers in this book and have received immediate relief from pain and sickness. Amazingly, a few days later, they find themselves back to square one and say, 'Oh, it didn't really work.'

Actually, it did really work but the thief came to steal their health again and they didn't stand against him in faith. This issue of healing is spiritual warfare – we cannot be half-hearted and expect Satan to run away.

> "...Resist the devil and he will flee from you."
> James 4:7

> "Resist him, steadfast in the faith..."
> 1 Peter 5:9

As in normal warfare, a constant bombardment is hard to resist and can make us crumble. That is why we need to constantly bombard Satan with the word of God and our faith in it.

As we resist him in this way, he will crumble. If we don't resist him, we will crumble and give in to sickness.

When I began to get some revelation of healing, Satan attacked my wife with sickness. It was a skin irritation that went on for nearly a year. The doctor was at a loss to explain it. I wondered if I had brought back some strange disease from Africa. We had to keep coming against that illness in faith. The temptation to give up was immense. But it was just not acceptable to resign ourselves to the idea that Hazel would suffer for the rest of her life. We fought on in prayer. Eventually, we discovered it was a rare infection and I am glad to say that Hazel has been well for many years now.

When we receive Jesus as our Lord and Saviour, we trust him in our heart and confess that faith with our mouth. It is a foregone conclusion that we will get to heaven because of receiving what Jesus did for us on the cross. That is our confident expectation.

We must adopt this attitude in the area of healing as well. And when we receive a healing through believing and speaking God's word, we must keep that healing the same way.

> "As you have therefore received Christ Jesus the Lord, so walk in him..."
> Colossians 2:6

If the symptoms come back, have some

warfare with Satan through God's word in your mouth. Notice that in the temptation of Jesus, he overcame Satan with the word of God. Every time he replied to the devil's attacks he said, "It is written..." and then quoted from the Bible (Matthew 4). If Jesus needed to speak the word of God to get the victory, how much more do we.

We need to treat sickness as though it was a snake climbing up our leg. If that happened we would take immediate and aggressive action and we wouldn't stop until the snake was dealt with.

If a snake was climbing up your leg, I don't think you would say, 'Oh Lord, if it by your will, take this snake from me. If not give me grace to suffer the snake bite...' No! I think you would shout at the snake, pull it off you and beat it until it was dead.

In Mark 11:23, Jesus didn't say we should talk to God about the mountain. He said we should speak to the mountain and tell it to be removed. We have to take authority over sickness and then make sure the 'snake' that attacked us is dead. I think we need to declare our healing and freedom from sickness almost daily. We have to establish some ground in the spirit. We have to set a boundary for Satan that he is not allowed to put sickness or disease back on us.

Of course, when Satan returns to put back on us a sickness we got free from, he uses all our memory of how unpleasant and persistent that sickness was. This is his tactic of intimidation. This is why we must constantly meditate on the fact that Jesus is bigger than all our problems and sickness. That the name of Jesus is above every name! We must have the mindset of young David when he approached Goliath. Goliath was big. But David knew that God was bigger.

We tend to get in our lives what we give our attention to. This is why our attention must be on Jesus and his word daily. Giving attention to God's word on a daily basis brings healing to our bodies.

> "My son, give attention to my words;
> incline your ear to my sayings.
> Do not let them depart from your eyes;
> keep them in the midst of your heart;
> for they are life to those who find them,
> and health to all their flesh."
>
> Proverbs 4:20-22

Divine healing, like the rest of our Christian walk, needs to be a lifestyle, not a brief season of interest. We need to learn, know and meditate on healing scriptures. We need to hear the word of God and stir up our faith all the time. We should seek repeated renewal of our faith.

St Paul urged young Timothy to do this. I don't know what happened to Timothy. Did his faith cool off? Did he lack spiritual power or fervour? We don't know, but evidently Paul saw his young friend had a problem and that the answer was in Timothy's own hands.

> "Therefore I remind you to stir up the gift of God which is in you through the laying on of my hands."
>
> 2 Timothy 1:6

Timothy was to 'stir up' or, as another translation puts it, 'rekindle' his faith.

I strongly suggest you re-read this book over and over until your faith in God's word drops into your heart. May God bless you as you believe God for your complete healing in body, mind and spirit.

Chapter 15

What about those who don't get healed?

Before ending this look at healing, I want to address a question I am asked often. What about those who don't get healed? I hesitate to include this chapter because some will use it to undermine everything else I have written. However, the question is asked so often I feel it needs to be addressed head-on.

Firstly, let me say that we should never give up praying for healing. There may be many challenges and set-backs but everyone I know who got their breakthrough, decided at some point in their story never to give up.

When I was training for the ministry, I had a practical placement every Tuesday in Bexley Mental Hospital. The building was one of the large old asylums built in the Victorian era. I worked with the chaplain, a lovely gentle man called Hugh, who seemed to have endless patience. Everyone in that place seemed to have a very short attention span. People shouted, wept, laughed, rocked and swayed.

Our main task was to hold a short service, sing a few hymns, read the Bible and preach a short word. I have never ministered in a more chaotic environment. Initially, I couldn't see how the gospel of Jesus would make any impact there. But we did see the kingdom of God come here and there. We did lay hands on those who asked for prayer, but often they were not asking for healing of their main problem of mental health but smaller issues and temporary physical symptoms. Yet every week, when I left at the end of the day, the patients were not healed.

Reflecting on that period, I think there were a few things going on in that place. Some people had a chemical imbalance that caused their mental disturbance. Others had been through a traumatic experience and had not recovered. Life's difficulties had worn others out emotionally. And I have no doubt that a few of them were under an attack of Satan and his demons. Nevertheless, we preached the word and prayed for those who asked, but many stayed sick.

For many years, I prayed for the sick and saw only small miracles and glimmers of God's healing power. Headaches and mild back pain being relieved.

It seems to me that we are broken people in

a broken world. And even those of us who have found Christ and have been restored, still carry a lot of baggage from our past. Rather than wondering why some are not healed, I am always amazed that anyone gets healed at all!

If we look back to the early Church, when many, many people got healed as the kingdom of God expanded, you will see there was persistent sickness around those who were used by God to heal. Peter healed many people in one place just by his shadow falling on them. On another occasion, the crowd tried to worship Paul and Barnabas as gods because of the power of God ministered through them.

Yet when we look at Paul's letters, there were obviously members of these missionary teams who got ill. That they were prayed for, I think, is implied. Yet some of them remained sick.

Paul's friend Epaphroditus was sick and nearly died. Eventually, he recovered and Paul attributes that eventual recovery to God's mercy (Philippians 2:26).

Another companion of Paul was Trophimus. After failing to get him healed, Paul left without him, leaving him on his sick bed in Miletus (2 Timothy 4:20).

Paul wrote to his young friend Timothy about

his frequent health problems.

> "No longer drink only water, but use a little wine for your stomach's sake and your frequent infirmities."
>
> 1 Timothy 5:23

So we are wrong to think that in those Bible days everyone on the ministry team always got healed and floated around on a cloud of God's blessing. No, they were real people like us, with real problems, difficulties and sickness from time to time.

More recently, I was ministering on a weekend healing mission in Blackpool. As the weekend approached I became ill. I had a temperature, headaches, a sore throat, running nose and a rasping cough. I had to preach four times over that weekend. Every service was a challenge and I spent the time between the services trying to sleep and recover my strength.

Yet when I prayed for the sick, we saw dramatic healing miracles! I contacted my friend Roy Todd who was ministering healing in another part of the country. He was surprised to hear my story, as he too was really ill as he ministered healing to others and saw the same level of miracle healings.

We were both asking the same question: How

does that work, God? The guy who's ministering healing... is sick!?

But we also both concluded that you have to press on by faith. We were not unaware of Satan's attack as, a couple of days after the missions, we both made a full and swift recovery.

So, to the question, 'Why are some not healed?' the short answer is, we don't know. But that question is not properly formed. It should be 'What about those who are not healed yet?'

It's never right to give up hope and stop praying. There is always hope and though sometimes it takes a while to come, I will keep repeating - healing is coming!

Life comes in seasons and it seems that sometimes miracles and healings are a distant memory. There are moments when we wonder where God is.

> "We are given no miraculous signs; no prophets are left, and none of us knows how long this will be. How long will the enemy mock you, O God? Will the foe revile your name forever? Why do you hold back your hand, your right hand? Take it from the folds of your garment and destroy them! But you, O God, are my king from of old; you bring salvation upon the earth. It was you who split

open the sea by your power; you broke the heads of the monster in the waters. It was you who crushed the heads of Leviathan and gave him as food to the creatures of the desert. It was you who opened up springs and streams; you dried up the ever-flowing rivers. The day is yours, and yours also the night; you established the sun and moon. It was you who set all the boundaries of the earth; you made both summer and winter."

Psalm 74:9-17 (NIV)

What I love about the psalmist's words is that, even when the miracles haven't come, we should still hope in God. He is our hope, our healing and the only one who can restore us.

"Though it tarries, wait for it;
because it will surely come,
it will not tarry."

Habakkuk 2:3

We live in the world of 'instant' and 'now'. But when you think about it, everything of value takes a little time to come.

"For yet a little while, and he who is coming will come and will not tarry."

Hebrews 10:37

We must be people who never quit. We must fight on and press through in faith. Though the road is sometimes long and hard, God is on our side and he will fight for us. We must remember what God has done, time and again for his people. Even when the odds seem overwhelming and the deck looks stacked against us, we must stir our faith in our Saviour.

> "When you go to war against your enemies and see horses and chariots and an army greater than yours, do not be afraid of them, because the LORD your God, who brought you up out of Egypt, will be with you. When you are about to go into battle, the priest shall come forward and address the army. He shall say: 'Hear, O Israel, today you are going into battle against your enemies. Do not be faint-hearted or afraid; do not be terrified or give way to panic before them. For the LORD your God is the one who goes with you to fight for you against your enemies to give you victory.'"
>
> Deuteronomy 20:1-4

When we go out against Satan to destroy his work of sickness, it is a battle. But God loves faith-filled children and he will fight for you. Be confident in that. 'Do not be faint-hearted or afraid; do not be terrified or give way to panic before them.'

Chapter 16

Ready, willing and able

To listen to some people talk, you'd think that God may heal the odd headache but he's not able to heal things like cancer or blindness. Yet listen to a different group of Christians and you would think that God is able to heal those things but he's sometimes not willing. Still others may say God is willing and able but he's not ready. If people would only look at the Bible, they would see these ideas are simply not true.

Firstly, let's consider if God is ready. According to Ecclesiastes 3:1, "There is a time for everything, and a season for every activity under heaven". So are we in the season when God is ready to heal?

After Jesus rose from the dead he appeared to his followers and commissioned them. He had already commissioned them to preach the gospel and heal the sick as they worked with him. But now a new season was opening up. They were commissioned to take this kingdom of God and its power into all the world to change lives.

A new season started on the Day of Pentecost as the Holy Spirit was poured out on ordinary people. The book of Acts traces the explosion of the Church from that day and the increase in miracles and healing. That season continues to this day. God is ready. Jesus declared to his followers:

> "And these signs will follow those who believe: In my name they *will* ... lay hands on the sick, and they *will* recover."
>
> Mark 16:17, 18

God said to Jeremiah:

> "...I am *ready* to perform my word."
>
> Jeremiah 1:12

God has repeatedly declared his intention to heal in his word. It is clear then that God is ready to perform his word.

Secondly, is God willing to heal? If you read through the gospels, you will not find any account of Jesus refusing to heal anyone. One particular man asked Jesus the very question we are looking at - is God willing to heal? The man was covered with leprosy.

> "...a man who was full of leprosy saw Jesus; and he fell on his face and implored him, saying, 'Lord, if you are willing, you can make me clean.' Then he put out his hand and touched him, saying, 'I am willing; be cleansed.' Immediately the leprosy left him."
>
> Luke 5:12,13

The God who revealed himself as '*Jehovah rapha*' is obviously willing to heal. The four gospels and the Acts of the Apostles are shot through with accounts of healing miracles performed by Jesus and his disciples. This convinces me beyond doubt that God is both ready and willing to heal you. He is ready. He is willing. But is he able?

Simply by virtue of being God, surely he must be able. Isaiah declared"

> "Surely the arm of the LORD is not too short to save, nor his ear too dull to hear."
> Isaiah 59:1 (NIV)

In other words, if there is a problem, it is not at God's end. Sometimes, particularly if we are very sick or have suffered a long illness, it is difficult to even imagine being free. It can be difficult to imagine God overcoming the mountain of illness that seems so big and overwhelming. When Paul wrote to his friends in what is now Turkey, he had a revelation – that God was far bigger than our problems and we could never comprehend what God could do or how he could do it.

> "Now to him who is *able* to do exceedingly abundantly above all that we ask or think, according to the power that works in us."
> Ephesians 3:20

God is able! Able not only to do what we are asking for, but ‘exceedingly abundantly above all that we ask or think’. That is more than we can imagine. So imagine the most amazing thing that could ever happen to you. Well God can do far more than that! He is able!

He is ready. He is willing. He is able. Sickness is going. Healing is coming!

A prayer for healing

Use this prayer daily for healing and to stir up your faith. The prayer is based on God's word so we know it is his will. Even if you don't feel like you believe it as you pray, persist as faith often comes as we hear God's word coming out of our own mouth.

> Thank you Jesus that you took my sickness and bore my infirmity.
> Today I will say 'I am strong!'
> Thank you that by your stripes I am healed.
> Thank you that you forgive all my sin and heal all my diseases.
> Thank you that the name of Jesus is above every name - above the name of sickness.
> At your name, every knee must bow.
> So today I command this sickness to bow before you.
> I curse and destroy every sickness and disease in my body in Jesus' name.
> I thank you that you make everything new.
> Holy Spirit, come now and touch me and make me whole and healed in my body, mind and spirit.
> I receive my healing now. Thank you Jesus.
> Amen.

Listen to Don online at
www.doneganpodcast.co.uk

other books by Don Egan

available from
www.rsvptrust.co.uk

Beautiful On The Mountains

The autobiography of Don Egan, founder of the RSVP Trust. When tragedy struck it looked like it was all over. But then an amazing opportunity opened up in Africa to transform thousands of lives.

"The moving story of an ordinary man following the extraordinary call of God. A joyful and tearful roller-coaster that will cause you to reflect about your own life."

J.John

Spiritual Detox

"Toxic attitudes and actions have polluted our lives and relationships and we think if we just detox our bodies we will be healthier - Don Egan has hit the nail on the head in this refreshing and relevant book to help us detox our minds, hearts and our souls."

J.John

A Word about your healing

Did you know there is a medicine so powerful, it can cure every sickness and disease known to mankind. It has no harmful side effects even when taken in large doses.

'A Word about your healing' shows how to enforce your healing through the word of God and prayer.

About the author

Don Egan is a Christian speaker, writer and missionary. He was commissioned by the Archbishop of Canterbury in 1987 and is also recognised by the Archbishops of York and Canterbury as a Member of the College of Evangelists. He has been in full time ministry in the Anglican Church for more than two decades.

He has spoken to hundreds of thousands of people throughout the UK, Europe, Asia and Africa. He is a regular speaker at conferences, churches and other events.

His main subject is faith for breakthrough - particularly in physical healing. He has witnessed many healings during his times of ministry including the blind seeing and the lame walking.

> 'It has been a delight to have known Don Egan for many years. Don is a man of character and integrity. He exudes the peace and presence of Christ and has the anointing of God on his life and ministry.'
>
> **Canon J John**
>
> *The Philo Trust*